Hey Christian lady, What is wrong with my makeup?

____

Written by Nicola Bright

Hey Christian lady, what is wrong with my makeup?

Dedication

- o This book is dedicated firstly to the LORD,- Thank you for being my all in all.
- o Second dedication goes to my wonderful husband - Thank you for loving and standing beside me no matter what. I love you so much.
- o Third dedication goes to the body of Christ.- Thanks to all my brothers and sisters in the Lord, your prayers and love means everything to me.

Table of Contents

4

Introduction

At the age of 16 where most young girls are self-conscious and insecure, is where you find me.

Most teenage girls get lost in the supposed glamour of movies, TV and magazines. A standard set forth by a culture obsessed with beauty. Our culture depicts and dictates what beauty is and isn't.

Most growing girl's crossover into womanhood fully influenced by one of the above-mentioned media outlets. Our media paints a picture of what is acceptable and what isn't. The social norms of our society herald's women liberties while simultaneously subjugating and objectifying them with sexual overtones and insecurities. All want to be accepted and seen as beautiful and our teens and baby girls are not exempt.

Chapter One

As a teen at the threshold of womanhood, I too wanted to fit in and find my acceptable place in society. I looked around me at what was acceptable and normal for women and consequently wanted to look and be like the women I saw. Society pushes a false sense of beauty and perfection as if what you have isn't good enough or no good at all. It is a subtle but dangerous concept, breeding self-hate or self-worship in women. You aren't up to standard; therefore, you need to change to fit the molded lie propagated by TV, magazines and movies. Subsequently, I went out and purchased for myself a lipstick and proceeded to wear it. As time went on, I started to notice the eyeliners of the women I admired, so I went out and bought some eyeliner as well, from there on, I noticed the well-defined eyebrows on these women and how well they were shaped. I was determined to have the same. These women were glorified and regarded by society as the most beautiful. A young, impressionable mind then gives way to the idea that this is how you get honor, attention and respect. Next, I bought a razor blade so I could further hone and shape my eyebrows to better fit the ever-changing mold I viewed many women flaunting. My first use of the blade, in so much anticipation of chiseling my brows into perfect shape, ended in horror. Not more than a second or two into sculpting my right brow, I somehow managed to remove half of it. So, unskilled was I. Through the fear of looking odd, I immediately decided to just go ahead and remove the complete eyebrow and its counterpart as well. I opted to draw them both in as it was better than any alternative I could think of at the time. I could then make them perfect. It looked a bit awkward at first but shortly thereafter I got used to it. Over time I became acquainted with the dark hues against my natural caramel skin and loved the contrasts. From that time on I started to pluck out the little stubs of regrown hair that threatened to ruin the perfect lines I'd come to master and create each morning.

As I grew and matured, I started to incorporate varied colored eye shadows, mascara, foundation and blushes into my makeup regimen. Though I only wore a full face of makeup when I was going out on special occasions, eyebrow pencil, eyeliner and mascaras were a normal staple for everyday applications. As the years went on and my affair with makeup continued, sometimes I would end up falling asleep in my beloved eyeliner and mascara. Makeup became a necessary and habitual staple in my life. I had a 12" x 12" makeup box and small makeup bags for my purse and car. These small bags all held eyeliners, eyebrow pencils, mascaras and a possible lipstick. I didn't think twice about using these things, they became and were second to nature and a necessary part of getting dressed daily. I loved my makeup and honestly never really wanted to be seen without some form of it on. Part of me felt as if I wouldn't be accepted without it. Makeup became such a part of me, I never thought twice about using it and later on becoming a model only helped to solidify my love for it.

Forward some 20 years later and keep in mind, that up to this point, I had been a born again Christian for about 14 years. Never, during those 14 years did I question my usage of makeup;

essentially never paying it any mind. I wore makeup daily to work and church for many years without an issue. I've heard testimonies of individuals regarding makeup but I never really gave weight to any of it. Makeup was a necessity for me.

I finally gave birth to my second child, a bouncing baby girl and instantly fell in love with her. Watching her grow I became amazed when her eyelashes started to bloom. She was perfect to me. God blessed me with this gem and I admired her throughout. I thought to myself; GOD gave her to me and I want her to live for HIM as she grew. I wanted to be her living example in all ways and manner. I wanted to hide her from the hurts and fears of the world. For the 1st time, I started to question where this idea of makeup and beauty came from because my little one was perfect in my sight and needed no makeup at all. Her face and all little children's faces as well, (as I now took great notice of) radiates glory. They are beautiful as they are. As a Christian woman, I started to feel objectified and subjugated by the idea of always having to put on makeup. God started to do a work in my heart. One day, I had a meeting at work. A group of selected personnel from different locations gathered to work on implementing a new company-wide system. It was a daunting effort that would take strong contributions from different departments (containing different talents and business domain experts) across the company to get it up and running by a set date. On this day, there was a young lady that sat a short distance to my right and I couldn't stop staring at her. I discovered, after some minutes why. She wore no makeup at all: no eyeliner, lipstick, foundation, blush, nothing. Yet, from the tone of her skin, I could tell that she was a person, as I, who was an avid user of makeup and possibly just recently stopped; or at least, was unable to put it on that day. The following consecutive days, she came to work maintaining the same look; makeup-free. I admired what I saw; she wore a natural face and yet was still confident and not lacking in her character. She wasn't self-conscious in any way that I could discern. It didn't seem to bother her as she boldly contributed her ideas. I wondered within myself if she realized she didn't have makeup on, as if; her having on makeup permits her to be confident and bold. Nonetheless, I loved her simplicity. Her look was clean and refreshing. I thought she was absolutely, beautiful and I admired it. I thought to myself, "What freedom, how nice it must be, to not be concerned or care to live up to the social pressures and standards of being beautiful and/or looking good." She was quite comfortable in her skin and didn't care if anyone else thought it was perfect or not.

Bach home, I looked deep into the eyes of my 10-month-old daughter and I saw nothing but beauty. To me, she was the most gorgeous thing I've ever laid eyes on. I didn't want her to ever change, nor feel pressured to cover up her GOD given beauty. From that point on, I started to take notice of men and how comfortable they were in their skin. They loved the way they were and felt no need to wear makeup, even shunning it. They enjoyed the face that God gave them, they don't feel pressured or less because they don't have makeup on. I started to admire such liberties. So, with this new-found admiration, I decided to stop wearing lipsticks, and then I gave up mascara. Eyeliner quickly followed and dropped off my list and finally, the hardest of all to give up; my most beloved eyebrow pencil. I always felt that my eyebrows were too light to go without darkening and now that I've shaved down my brows to barely being there, how could I give up my brow pencil. It was hard but I so wanted to taste the freedom I witnessed in others. God placed a hunger in me concerning this. I started to think hard and long about how women have become addicted to makeup without even realizing it. We no longer feel pretty without a little something on. It's like a mental epidemic that has poisoned both the young and the old. I started to think about the psychological effects it has on our little girls growing up, how when they're small we tell them they are cute and adorable but when they get older, they are no longer cute and need to alter their look to achieve this. The unsaid statement/message that can be felt by all young girls is that "To be beautiful you must change". Society tells them they aren't beautiful anymore and need some stuff added to be beautiful and valued. They must change what they have and how they look to be accepted. They no longer want to resemble their parents, they feel the nose they got is wrong, the eyebrows they have aren't right. Their lips are not full or shaped correctly and their facial structures aren't quite correct. Overall, it seems they feel that they can't fit in being themselves and they have to change or enhance their look. The subliminal message is; "You are faulty and imperfect, change it to look like this or that." Some go to extreme measures and opt for surgery to accommodate the status quo. Merchandisers have even found a way to sell to us, in the form of makeup, what we already have; "The Natural Look." How absurd is this when you think of it logically.

Chapter Two

I began to think more and more on how I would feel if my little girl had my eyes, grew up and wanted to change them because she saw it as a flaw. I then started to think about how God must feel because we want to change HIS image and HIS likeness. The bible says: Genesis 1:26 Then God Said, "Let us make man in our image, after our likeness….   In GOD's infinite mind and unending wisdom, He decided that you would look the way you look. Your eyes would be set that way, your hair would be that way, your nose would be that way, etc. He wanted you to reflect and showcase another unique aspect of HIMSELF and His glory. You then decide that HIs work of creating you wasn't good enough. You weren't created perfect, so now, you strive to change the look He gave you. He took so much thought into making you that HE even counted the hairs on your head. Luke 12:7 "And even the very hairs of your head are all numbered…". My next thought was, this must break HIS heart in a million different ways. You were created uniquely down to your fingerprints.

I started to do some research to see how the church feels about makeup and I found out the church was divided on the topic. Some churches believe you should wear makeup and some churches believe you shouldn't. The bible never outright said that makeup was a sin but it is striking to know that the places it does mention makeup; it had a negative connotation and was associated with whorish/seductive behavior. Read: Jeremiah 4:30 - "And when thou art spoiled, what wilt thou do? Though thou clothest thyself with crimson, though thou deckest thee with ornaments of gold, though thou rentest thy face with painting, in vain shalt thou make thyself fair; thy lovers will despise thee, they will seek thy life." God is speaking of the harlotry of the church here. & Kings 9: 30-" And when Jehu was come to Jezreel, Jezebel heard of it; and she painted her face, and tired her head, and looked out at a window". Jezebel did this to seduce the man of GOD.

Thinking beyond this, I started to wonder then, what really was the problem with makeup because I just didn't have any peace in my heart about it. I then realized it was a heart condition. Most women wear makeup not because they have a real flaw but because it was the social norm and they wanted to fit in and be seen as beautiful or looking good. Looking back, I realized that I didn't wear makeup to hide my childhood scar that visibly displayed itself on my forehead. My scar never bothered me growing up or when I became an adult. I wore makeup for the same reasons most women around me did. Most wear makeup because they don't feel beautiful enough without it or they don't feel sexy. They don't feel seductive or confident without it and are mostly blind to the fact like I was for so many years. I find that women on a whole are addicted to it and it has become a necessary habit in their lives. Most women don't feel fully dressed up until they have makeup on. Ask yourself this: Can I go to a wedding, a ball, a meeting, the mall, work, or to church without makeup on? Some women have it so bad that their spouse never sees them without makeup on. Now, the problem is, as a Christian woman nothing is supposed to have this kind of control and hold over you, except GOD. If you are had by a thing, you have a stronghold and it needs to be dealt with. This creates weaknesses in you and leaves you susceptible to the attacks of your enemy. You are only as strong as your weakest point like a chain is only as strong as the weakest link. Anything that controls you, is your god! Your identity should not be found in makeup but in GOD.

A deeper look at your motives is necessary. Are there any hidden gaps and/or weaknesses behind you wearing makeup? Maybe you hadn't thought about it before now. Did someone tell you, you needed it to "Look good" or to "Look better"? And you believed them? That's a self-confidence and self-esteem issue. Your battle is in the mind. Is it that you think you need it, to be beautiful? Is it a fleshly/carnal issue you are having? Is it pride of life? Do you have a heart issue? Do you desire to be looked at/ be admired? Is it a self-glorification/self-idolatry problem you are having? Do you want to look sexy and if so, why? Is it for the attention of men and if so, why? Do you seek to impress people for their praises and if so, why? Do you have a lust or pride issue? Are you just trying to fit in and if so, why? You must search your heart to find out these things. You have to sit down and ask yourself some real serious questions and weigh it to see if it is putting your salvation in jeopardy. When you start to search your heart about these things you start to see how easily it besets you and how it leaves open doors in your life. Your main concern should be; am I right before GOD? Does the enemy have any legality in my life to ruin it? Most women cannot get up and walk outside, much less, get dressed up for an occasion and not put on makeup at all. What is wrong with this picture? It's as if it's a mental poison. Who lied to us about beauty and what it means to be beautiful? Who is responsible for setting forth the standards of beauty? Where did we get these distorted ideas of beauty? Where did it come from and why do we follow them so sheepishly and never question the whys? Some women can't stand to look at themselves in the mirror without makeup, which is a problem. A woman should know that she is beautiful with or without makeup. She shouldn't have self-hate. A woman should feel comfortable in her skin and not feel less or pressured if she steps out in her GOD given glory. GOD would never cover you up. HE loves you because to HIM, you are perfect and the most beautiful thing HE ever laid eyes on and/or created. You are truly priceless as you are. You are a part of HIM and carry HIS glory.

It appears that we are creating a kind of sick society that breeds little girls that hate themselves, all the while looking for perfection but never seeing that they are already perfect. We train our little girls to be insecure teens that become insecure women, who hate themselves. We are so liberated but still enslaved.

Chapter Three

The main point is this, if you wear makeup, you need to search yourself and make sure you aren't using it to cover up a bigger problem. Inferiority, insecurity, fear of rejection, vanity, idolatry, seduction, jealousy, deception, acceptance, addiction, self-esteem issues, pride, etc. Search your soul and if you find out that you are indeed hiding a bigger problem, pray and take the necessary steps you need to heal.

God will heal every hurt, every pain, every wound, every failure, you only need but ask.

Chapter Four

* * *

If you don't have a relationship with GOD and would like to, believe in your heart and pray this prayer:

"Dear Jesus, please forgive me of all my sins and come into my heart and have a relationship with me, I want to know you. In Jesus name! Amen."

If you prayed the prayer above, welcome to the family of GOD!

Get a bible and start reading it from the book of Mark and ask GOD to lead you to a church where HE is, so you can grow spiritually.

Chapter Five

~ My Prayer for you ~

Father in heaven, please touch every woman and girl that took the time to read this book and have set their hearts to seek out the things that please you. I ask you to restore the natural beauty and tones of the skin in those who decide to give up makeup, I pray that you restore the hair follicles of those who have lost them due to years of abuse, let the hair grow where it has stopped growing. Lord, I ask you to stand beside all these women and let them see the beauty in themselves and the beauty you see in them. Father, I ask that you heal all the hurts, failures and brokenness that may exist in the hearts of those that have read this book. Father, I love you and thank you for touching your people, in JESUS name I pray. Amen